THE VOICE OF
UNIVERSAURIUS
AND
LIFETRONS

A COSMIC MOVEMENT FOR THE PLANET EARTH

UNIVERSARIUN FOUNDATION

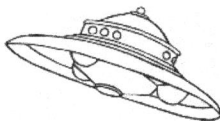

SAUCERIAN PUBLISHER

ISBN: 978-1-955087-09-4

9 781955 087094

© 2022, Saucerian Publisher

PROLOGUE

It is generally a good idea to return to the classics in any genre. This also goes for UFO literature. Rereading a book, or reviewing old documents after ten or twenty years is a rewarding experience. You will discover new data and ideas you didn´t notice before. The reason, of course, is that you are, in many ways, not the same person reading the book the second or third time. Hopefully you have advanced in knowledge, experience, intellectual and spiritual discernment. A good starting point is to reread the contactee classics material of the 1960s, in order to understand the deeper mystery involved in what happened during that era.

Classic UFO contact, like George Van Tassel, George Adamski involves the physical interaction between humans and otherworldly beings. However, other evidence that mainstream ufologists have commonly ignored is "transcendental communication", "mental radio," which today is widely called "channelers". Over the years, these paranormal people have been ignored.

The Universariun Foundation was formed in 1958 and for many years headquartered in Portland, Oregon. Among the small group, Zelrun Karsleigh and his wife, Daisy Karsleigh, then still in her teens, began to receive telepathic material. Meetings were held regularly in their home, and the work grew steadily. For several decades, the Karsleighs remained the primary channels of messages from the spirit world, though eventually others have developed within the group.

Messages have been received from both the ascended masters and the masters from outer space. The principle communicators have been Sri Soudah, Koot Hoomi, and Lord Michael. The material follows the perspective of the "I AM" Religious Activity and is aimed at the illumination and emancipation of earth from its fear, chaos, and confusion.

The Universariun Foundation was governed by a board of

seven directors elected by the membership at an annual meeting. The board oversees publication of the monthly periodical. A sanctuary for weekly meditation and telepathic channeling and a bookstore were maintained in Tucson. The recommended reading list of books, sold on a mail-order basis, include a wide variety of metaphysical works.

The 70-page booklet *The Voice of Universarius and Lifetrons,* published in April, 1967, by Universariun Founsation is a collection of lectures and short discourses received by "mental radio" from MASTER YOGUNDA, a master in space, in another vibration of life.

Saucerian Publisher was founded to promote Flying Saucer, Paranormal, and the Occult books. Our vision is to preserve the legacy of literary history by reprinting editions of books that have already been exhausted or are difficult to obtain. Our goal is to help readers, educators, and researchers by bringing back original publications that are difficult to find at a reasonable price while preserving the legacy of universal knowledge. This title is an authentic reproduction of the original Universariun Foundation's *The Voice of Universarius* . This book is a facsimile reproduction of the original printed text in shades of gray. Because this material is culturally important, we have made it available as part of our commitment to protect, preserve and promote knowledge in the world. This book has been formatted from their original version for publication. **IMPORTANT, although we have attempted to maintain the integrity of the issues accurately, the present reproduction could have missing and blurred pages poor pictures due to the age of the original scanned copy.** Because this material is culturally important, we have made it available as part of our commitment to protect, preserve and promote knowledge in the world.

This title has the following contensts: GATEWAY TO LIFE; MASTER YOGUNDA; MASTER YOGUNDA, Discourse #128; MASTER YOGUNDA, Discourse #129 ; SANANDA; MASTER YOGUNDA, Discourse #130; MASTER YOGUNDA, Discourse #131; NEWS ITEMS; BOOK LIST; VANITY FAIR - Song by RM. Balz .

Editor, Saucerian Publisher, 2022

THE VOICE OF

UNIVERSARIUS
AND
LIFETRONS

A COSMIC MOVEMENT FOR THE PLANET EARTH

VOLUME 6	APRIL 1967	NUMBER 4

TABLE OF CONTENTS

oooooooooooooooooooooooooooooooooooooooooooooooooo
oooooooooooooooooooooooooooooooooooooooooooooooooo

Subscription Rates: $10.00 per year in advance; $1.00 per month
or $3.00 per quarter if paid in installments. Ten issues a year.
Monthly except Bi-monthly Aug.-Sept. and Oct.-Nov.

UNIVERSARIUN FOUNDATION, INC.
3620 S.E. 84th Avenue, Portland, Oregon 97266

SECOND CLASS MATTER - POSTAGE PAID AT PORTLAND, OREGON

Florence Azlo Karsleigh
(1882-1967)

IN MEMORIAM

Florence Azlo Karsleigh was born May 23, 1882 at Markesan, Wisconsin.

At 17, she was married at Kenemere, N.D. to Charles A. Meyers. Three girls were born of this union, Gladys, Hazel and Lila.

She was a rural mail carrier in North Dakota for 11 years while her husband operated the farm. They established the first Star Route out of Kenemere and the first Rural Route out of Tolly. Much of the winter driving was in sub-zero weather and blinding snow storms, but delivery was always made.

She joined the Congregational Church at Maple Lake, Minn. when 14 and was a member of the First Congregational Church here in Portland. She came to Portland in 1929.

She was very active in Technocracy in its early days. She was a member of the Jane Jefferson Democratic Club, The S.E. Women's Democratic Club, Friends of The Aged, and was interested in many activities of the Church.

After her marriage to Zelrun Karsleigh on July 18, 1957, she became interested and assisted in the work of The Universariun Foundation, Inc.

Mrs. Karsleigh made her transition June 23rd at the Multnomah County Hospital from a kidney infection from a fractured hip sustained on February 6 of this year.

She is survived by her husband, a daughter, a sister, two brothers, many grandchildren, great-grandchildren and great-great-grandchildren.

Funeral services were held June 27 at The Little Chapel of The Chimes here in Portland. Interment at Sunset Hills Cemetery.

DEATH, GATEWAY TO LIFE

Let us consider the mission of death. Millions through the ages have beheld him with terror. Let us dispel the gloom. O Death, thou givest a brother liberty, a more glorious freedom to the soul.

The door of thy castle swings inward, noislessly opening upon enchanted chambers, radiant with unwonted Light and Glory, such as Earth has never known.

Thou kisseth down the eyelids in sleep, O Death, and dost imprint upon the lips the seal of immortality, Beautiful, indeed at thy gentle touch hath been the awakening into new experiences........not into a new life, but into a new individual experience for it is the same life that has unfalteringly kept its march through the ages, and thou bringest its fuller realization.

New fields, O Human Soul, lie open before thee and loftier heights than ever, thy feet have scaled stretch up and on before thee.

Death hath not robbed thee of thy treasures All the good thou hast done, all the noble thoughts thou hast expressed, live and are with thee still. O Death, thou holdest within thy hands the key which unlocks the door of space and time.

Art thou bereft of friends and loved ones? Doth sorrow rest heavily upon thy aching head? Doth thy tired spirit seek for rest? Thou art not alone. Thy friends and loved ones were never so near to thee as now. All the fetters are broken and thy friends can draw nearer to thee now than ever before.

The sweet communion of spirit with spirit shall cool thy fevered, aching brow and assuage thy lurking sorrow. Thy heart bowed down shall beat again with lightness and with ecstasy.
(Continued Page 64)

MASTER YOGUNDA

11th Chapter, Revelations   May 24, 1967

GGGGG REETINGS and Salutations, Beloved Ones
G GG   of Light. I was concerned whether or
GGGGG   not I could impress upon our Channel
the words I desire to give him in the manner
which has been established. I am delighted
that the vibrations generated are   more
spontaneous than sometimes innprevious meetings.

        My Beloved Ones, I thank you for the vib-
rations which you have created here tonight
by your presence and by your thought forms
which have emanated into this room, into this
city and this nation and all the world. This
has created a happy feeling among all of us.

        I AM now broadcasting my messages to you
from my home upon the Spiritual Realm. It
is not within my province, except on special
occasions, to come in person to speak to you,
and that you may be able to see me. Some, of
course, will sense my presence, and perhaps
even see in the aura of our Channel the manifestations of the Light upon which I am coming, into his presence and yours.

        This evening, I greet you with Love and
Understanding and I also greet you with Peace
and Joy. It is a joy to me that I have been
able to continue this steadfast rapport with
you throughout all these months.

        You do not realize the joy of all those
in the Heavenly Realms, the Etheric World,
not only where I reside, but others as well,
 that these messages can be transmitted
through a human channel. The most remarkable part is that you, My Beloved Chelas,
have made it possible to disseminate these
teachings throughout the world and to give
them to hundreds who are thirsting for right-

eousness, knowledge and understanding of life
and evolvement that takes place not only on
earth but in the heavens as well. Many times
I have tried to explain to you the mysteries
of life, and sometimes I have undertaken to
bring you interpretations of the Sacred Books,
not only your Biblical Scriptures, but others
as well.

This evening, I took upon myself a stu-
pendous undertaking in a way, yet it is simple
if it is analyzed properly. I did not know
the interpretation of some of my own Scriptures
in the Vedas until I received additional instruction upon the Higher planes or the spiritual realms.

This evening, in response to a promise
that I made, I will try to explain, if I may,
the Chapter of the Book of Revelation which
you have just read in my presence, and in
the presence of your assembly, and also in
the presence of those who are waiting to hear
from me. This will be a clarification of a
nebulous interpretation which has been made
by the Christian Orthodox Church. Most of the
leaders have skipped entirely this particular
chapter as well as other chapters of Revelation, because they could not understand it,
and therefore, no attempt has been made to
interpret it sufficiently that the Chelas of
Light and members of the Church could understand it.

There has been much written about it,
and you have two books which explain it in
a manner, but not perhaps as simply, nor as
completely as I hope to be able to do for
you this evening.

I will immediately go into the interpretation. First of all, what is the reed,
that has been described as a rod? This is
the word of God, or the Word that is coming

from God, and I use the word, God, in its entirety. If I would simply use the words --
Spiritual Hierarchy -- then I would be limit-
ing the scope of these words which are being
spoken to the Earth at this time. All that
represents enlightenment, evolvement and instruction is coming directly from God. I do
not mean by this statement that all words, or
all channels are directly connected with the
higher realms, for some of them are not as I
have told you before. Generally speaking,
this is true, and the volume of information
which is coming from the spiritual realms
would burden you to read and absorb it even
if you read only one percent of it.

So the reed is likened unto a rod. A rod
is something that is substantial; it is something that can be used to smite with and it
can be used as a support. This goes back to
the symbology of the olden days when these
things were written and were given to Beloved
John upon the Isle of Patmos -- Patmos being
interpreted as Peace. Peace is 'Patmos" in
the Greek language. Therefore, this was a place
of Peace where these Revelations were given. *

In the third verse of Chapter 11, it
speaks of the two witnesses. Does this mean
two individual people? Does it mean two leaders who will come forth as leaders in your New
Age? No. Definitely not! This passage has
confused and puzzled those who have read it.
The two witnesses are the two parts of man --
or the Alpha and Omega. This is a nebulous
phrase -- Alpha and Omega, being interpreted
as the beginning and end. The two witnesses
are the two parts of man -- his physical being,
and the Holy Spirit which is the Word of God
in his soul. Therefore, the two witnesses who
have come forth are not two individuals, but
 are the two parts of entire humanity upon the
earth who are bringing forth much information

6 -

and instruction.

"......They shall prophesy a thousand two
hundred and threescore days, clothed in sackcloth." There are those who prophesy and those
who do not prophesy, but bring forth only instruction and information such as I am bringing you. I have been very cautious in my prophecies as you will remember. I have given
you some prophecies which have already taken
place.

The two witnesses are not two individuals.
They are the two parts of man which is physical and spiritual. How could they come forth
if they were NOT in two parts? The physical
man cannot deliver to people of earth, spiritual truth. It must come from the Holy Spirit. Also it must come through the physical
instrumentality of man just as you are receiv-
ing this message this evening. If it were not
for his willingness to be a receiver of this
truth, if it were not for his voice, if it were
not for his physical anatomy, you would not be
able to receive the message and it would not
be brought to the people of earth. Now do you
understand? They are not humans but represent
the human race in general, or the prophets of
the New Age who are bringing forth this great
truth.

The two witnesses have power to smite
the earth with plagues. Naturally, they are
'plaguing" those who do not accept the Christ
teachings. This is the interpretation of the
plagues. The two witnesses are bringing forth
plagues -- not physical plagues, not frogs,
lice or mice, or boils such as were given the
Egyptians in the early days, but are plaguing
the minds and souls of those individuals who
will not accept the Christ Light, and teachings. Those who do not accept the teachings
are warring against the two witnesses, warring

against Truth, warring against the physical
and spiritual.

Many have been restrained and some have
been put in mental institutions becuase they
have been giving out information on Space, or
something about New Age teachings which con-
tradicted the old, orthodox teaching which
has been in force for centuries and centuries.
Therefore, they will fight against both the
physical and spiritual as well.

Will these two witnesses be killed? Yes,
of course, they will be killed, not in the
physical body, not in the spiritual body, but
the teachings will be killed for a time and
"lie in the street." However, they will not
be buried. The teachings which are coming
forth from hundreds and hundreds of sources,
whether they are channels of Light such as
this one, or whether they be books, or whether
they be proclaimed from the pulpit of the orthodox church -- these are Truths, and they
will be "killed," but they will not be buried.
They shall lie, so to speak, in the "street"
where all can see them. They cannot possibly
be buried because they are living. Even though
they may be spiritually killed, they are still
living and they are there for all to observe
and see.

These Truths are naked; they are forceful,
but even the Satanic forces -- forces of the
Evil One -- have at last been able to "kill",
or will be able in a short time, the forces
of Light which have been proclaiming Truth.
Truth cannot be buried, nor the Forces of Light
which will be very evident and they will lie in
wait for their resurrection. Does not the same
account tell you they will arise again from
the street and will curse and disdain those who
have tried to kill them? The Power of Light,
the Power of God will overcome those who have
actually "killed" them, in a sense.

In the Chapter there is a very beautiful portrayal of the New Age when the Power
of the Holy Spirit and the Power of God will
permeate all hearts of men, except those few
who remain. These remaining ones will tremble
and have fear as the account states because
these witnesses have been raised up before
their very eyes, they who had been castigated,
thrown down and "killed". The actual "killing"
of coUrse, was not a process of death, but a
state of dormancy until the time arrives when
Truth -- the two witnesses -- the human souls
who have been faithful, and who have been so
earnest in the proclamation of the Word, will
rise again from the Earth and proclaim the
Glories, the Riches of the Gospel of the New
Age of Christ Jesus Who will come, and has already come, to rule over the hearts and minds
of mankind.

I do not know what else I can give you
in regard to the interpretation of this particular passage for it has been rather nebulous and misinterpreted and given up as
unsolvable. The interpretation is simple if
we look for the hidden meaning. Most of the
Book of Revelation is presented in an alle-
gorical manner, symbolical of that which
could not be understood at the time, but will
be revealed and IS revealed in the latter
years.

Let us dwell briefly upon the numbers a
given. First, we have 42 months, then one
hundred and three score days which is the
same as 42 months which adds to three and
one-half years. This might be classified in
the category of prophecy, but I shall not
make it thus, for you already know part of
the conditions which transpired.

I will tell you in a moment why one was
specified in months and the other in days
which may be interesting to you.

So that I may not get ahead of my narrative, I will state briefly that as far as the present situation is concerned, the three and one-half years started approximately at the time I came to your group to give you messages through your channel in the early part of 1964. It will continue for three and one-half years from that time. THEN will come the tribulations, or the days specified in the second part and will continue from that time until approximately the year 1971 which completes a total of seven years, does it not?

Until this time you will have confusion, and chaos in the world according to the scriptures which was read. Now why did they specify in one place 42 months, and in another place the same length in days? This is very simple. In the preceding Dispensation, or the preceding years and months, things had been normal, let us say, yet, of course, events have been transpiring very rapidly. You have calculated time in months, but from this time forward -- from the end of this year, each day will bring an added crisis in the world and will bring you to a realization that every day in the ensuing months will be one of great consequence and one which you will look upon as a day of anxiety or day of achievement, whichever applies.

So the days will be counted. YOU WILL BE COUNTING THE DAYS, not months from the end of this year until 1971. You will be counting days, not weeks or months. Each new day will bring with it a new crisis or a new outlook upon life and the world in general.

With faith and understanding you must face those crucial days, and you must face it with greater faith, understanding and spiritual power than the preceding day.

I could interpret this a sort of prophecy, but I admonish you that the days coming which are specified in this passage of scripture are very important, not only to you, but to every human upon the face of the earth, and this is the reason the time is specified in days rather than months. This has been mysterious since the days, and the months, and the years total the same. In one case the months, and in another case the days, each bring a total period of seven years. There have been books written about this but they have not been entirely correct in their diagnosis of time.

Of course, I could give you another discourse upon Time, and the Timing. The Beloved Masters and I have given you lectures upon the subject of TIMING which is SO important in the evolution of a race and the progression of a planet.

Some of the timing has been delayed and some of it has been set forward, so prophetic events cannot be pinpointed at this time. This is the reason I am very reluctant to give you any prophecy, except as it enlightens you as to what you may expect in the forthcoming months and days.

This 11th Chapter of Revelations has been so nebulous, misunderstood, omitted and ignored even by the Orthodox Church because they could not interpret nor understand it.

Now if you have any questions about this chapter, perhaps about the months or days that are crucial at this time, I shall be glad to answer them for you. This concludes my explanation and exposition of this chapter.

Q: Thank you, Master Yogunda, from the very depth of my heart. Now I have a question: Now these two witnesses are given power to shut up the Heavens that it will not rain during this period. Does this mean a period of real spiritual famine upon the earth?

A: In a sense, it does mean this -- it does
not mean, of course, physical rain. You are
right in that it does mean a rain of spiritual
power. There are many of the phrases which I
did not mention. The Heavens will be shut up
during the time these two witnesses are lying
"dead" in the streets. Also water will be turned to blood. What does that mean? Does it mean
that water actually will be turned to blood?
No, certainly not. Water is symbolical of
purity and cleansing, is it not? Instead of
purity or cleansing, there shall be blood flowing, and there is blood flowing now, is there
not? You find this in all parts of the world,
not only in the Far East, but in other parts
of the world where blood flows freely. Blood
is also a symbol of evil, in a way. There are
two interpretations.

        Do you remember in Exodus Chap. 7, verse
20, for example when the waters were turned to
blood? Of course, you read in the scriptures
where the blood of Christ redeems the race from
its sins. These are the two opposites, but in
a sense, they mean the same thing. So the waters
shall be turned to blood which is being fulfilled at the present time.

        I think I can anticipate your next question
as I am reading your minds now. You are somewhat reticent to state your question as you do
not know how to phrase it. Therefore, I will
give you a brief prophecy -- that is what you
want. I hesitate to do this, but inasmuch as
this is something of interest to all, I shall
give it.

        In regard to the situation which is now
shaping between the two powers, Arab and Israel, I will tell you briefly that the crisis
is not over as yet. If you will check on this
you will find it to be correct. As you know,
the Arabians have placed explosives which are

termed mines, at the entrance to the Sea of
Acaba. There are two or three vessels headed
in that direction. One of these ships has
determined to enter this Strait and will try
to avoid the mines. It will be very difficult
to restrain them, and Israel is standing by
to see what the conditions will be. The Security Council of the United Nations will pre-
vail upon this vessel not to enter because
it would immediately precipitate a conflict,
a very bloody and far-reaching conflict between these two so-called smaller powers.

This is now held in abeyance and as you
have the expression, "the whole world is sit-
ting upon a powder keg." However, this powder
keg will not explode because of the efforts of
the Security Council of the United Nations.
This action, of course, is being influenced by
the Higher Powers, those who are overshadowing
the Council. This is one of the great forces
of evil which is being turned loose at the present time, in addition to the conflict in Viet
Nam. There will be no major conflict of major
importance, but there will be an incident which
could precipitate a full scale conflict, but it
will be subdued and held to a minimum by the
Higher Powers in the Spiritual Realm. Now does
this answer your questions you had in mind?

Q: Yes.

A: I anticipated both of them and therefore
I desired to give you this prophecy which you
might consider as good news, although it is
not resolved in its entirety.

Q: Master Yogunda, in a group the other day,
which we belong to, Alice Bailey came through
a channel. She is an Ascended Master now.
What is she doing?

A: Just one moment please. I could give you
information about many, many Masters whom you

have read about, and some whom you may know
personally through your spiritual contact
who are working together. I want to empha-
size this word, "together". This group you
are in, of course, is separate from your own
group, yet in a sense you are "together", for
all groups are together in a spiritual sense
in the spiritual realm.

Now my Beloved Colleague, Alice Bailey --
she was a colleague, although she did not
live during the full time of my own earthly
life, yet she was given a specific work to
do upon the earth plane. Her principal mission at the present time is Ambassador at
Large, in a manner great deal the same as
Master Sananda and Kuthumi and many others
who are working specifically with those Chelas
of Light who have studied the I AM, the Theo-
sophical approach to life, although her efforts
are not confined to these groups. She is working specifically with these and also that
type of assembly to whom she came at this particular time to inform you of her Love and
Light. Yes, her work is very widespread and
very important at this particular time along
with that of many of the Ascended Masters,
like Lady Nada, Kuthumi, Sananda and Leadbeater
I could include the Archangels, Michael, Gabriel, and many more that I could name. She is
one of them and she is on a very high rung
of spiritual evolvement.

Q: Master Yogunda, I would like to know if
you have any information as to how far my
husband has progressed and what he is doing
now and did he visit our group the other day.
I would like to know a little more about
where he is now and what he is doing?

A: I will answer your question and it portrays
the condition of many who are in the Spirit
World today.

He is making progress, but his progress
is slow. I mean by this that it is not unduly
slow, but that he is not in a position to make
rapid progress like some who are on that plane
are able to make. He is about in the same condition or situation that he was, but his teachers are insisting he spend more time in instruction instead of looking around so much.
He wants to find out about all the things which
are going on around him which is commendable,
yet he is neglecting some of the deeper things
and thoughts of life, and you can help him in
that matter if you will project your thoughts
and love to him. He is progressing, but it
is slow because he is scattering his energies
somewhat and .....which you do....very often
upon the earth!

Q: Master Yogunda, in a number of prophecies
that have come forth concerning the war in Viet
Nam, it says that it will stop almost overnight.
If this is true, will it be due partly to the
Middle East situation, diverting the attention
there rather than in Viet Nam?

A: It will not specifically have an effect,
although it will have a certain effect on it.
Due to the tensions divided between the Middle
East situation and Viet Nam, there will be much
greater pressures brought to bear upon both of
them. In Viet Nam the conflict will be shortened which will be brought about by an increased
awareness on the part of those who should be
aware of the implications in effect.

Greater power and energy will be manifest-
ed in India than has been shown until the present time. If you will remember, the war between India and Pakistan was brought to an almost sudden termination. This was due to the
tremendous power that India exerted in the de-
crees and thought forms. They will enter into
this conflict because it has a direct bearing
upon India and the countries adjacent to her.

Q: The Scriptures say in Matthew, Chapter 24,
 verse 22, "And except those days shall be shortened, there should no flesh be saved; but for
the elects sake those days shall be shortened."
Is this referring to the present or to the future?

A: This refers to the present and the immediate future. The conditions which have prevailed upon the planet in the last few years
have made it necessary that the days be shortened in order that man-made catastrophes might
not take place. This information I gave you in
a discourse some time ago called "The Fielder's
Choice," which dealt with the question whether you would rather have a natural or a man-
made destruction. This phrase is, however,
rather nebulous,but it simply means there will
be less days to the resolution of the chaos on
earth than there was before.

Q: I believe this is all the question for tonight, Master Yogunda, and we certainly have
enjoyed them.

A: Thank you. You have asked some good questions and I always enjoy answering them if possible. I think that I have been able to answer
most of them for you.

   I will now pronounce a benediction upon
you because of your faithfulness and because of
the fact that we have been together and have
been such wonderfully, good friends for all of
these months that I have been with you.

   God bless you. May the Father of Light,
the Father-Mother God bless and prosper you,
forever and ever, in great abundance.

   Amen.

   I AM Master Yogunda. Good night.

* * * * * * * * *

MASTER YOGUNDA

Discourse No. 128   Nov. 3, 1966

GREETINGS AND SALUTATIONS, my Beloved
Chelas of Light. Tonight, I would give you
more than salutations for I am very happy to
again see those faces of times past who have
listened to my humble discourses. I am always happy to renew the acquaintance of those
who have formerly been with us, dropped away,
and then returned.

I welcome each and every one of you this
evening into a high vibration of Love, Wisdom
and Power which you have brought with you. I
feel the vibration each time we gather together,
and sometimes it is very strong, sometimes it
is barely strong enough for me to come through.
Of course, as I have told you many times, I have
those invisible to you who help with the transmission. Therefore, we shall not fail to bring
you the message designated for a particular
time unless, of course, it is beyond our control.

Tonight, I am going to continue with my
explanation of the Universal Laws of the Cosmos. As I have told you, there is but ONE LAW,
and that is the Law of Cause and Effect, but
there are thousands of corollaries of this
one law. At our last transmission I gave you
something about the Law of Compensation. This
evening, I would like to speak about the Law
of De-compensation. This is a Universal Law
the same as the Law of Compensation.

I have treated the Law of Compensation from
a metaphysical, spiritual angle which I may
talk about tonight, but first I would like to
advise you upon the Law of Change. This Law applies to every phenomena, every manifestation,
every atom, every particle of creative material,
spirit, planet, galaxy or what have you in

the Universe as it is constituted. There
is no such thing in all such life as solid-
ityor that which does not change. Everything in the Universe eventually changes.

It may be somewhat difficult for the
human mind to apply this Law of Change to
a Solar System, a Planet, a Continent, riv-
ers, or mountains which you see every day.
You consider everything is fixed in their
locations and that they are permanent. Let
me assure you this evening there is no permanency in any of OM-NI-TORS creation.

Now perhaps, you may sense that I am
leading up to the Scripture which was read
here tonight. Many predictions and prophecies have come forth from many channels
and prophets in the past and are coming
forth in great profusion in regard to the
changes which are coming to the planet Earth.

In the past and in your own recorded
history there have been hundreds and thousands of changes, some minor, some major.
Some of these changes have been classified
by historians and those who do not have
the spiritual knowledge, as legends. They
are not legends, but have taken place at
one time or another in the unrecorded history of your planet.

Does it not, therefore, seem reasonable there will be other major changes, not
only to the topography of the planet Earth,
but to its inhabitants, its atmosphere, its
relationship with other planets in the Galaxy and even with the time element of its
orbital and daily revolutions. I would advise you to think deeply about the imminent
changes that are to take place upon the planet. I have used the word, 'IMMINENT" because
these changes which have been prophesied for
hundreds and thousands of years, are now imminent. They will be far-reaching in a very

marked degree. The inhabitants of the Earth will even be changed. Now what do I mean by change? I have given you, in times past, as has our Beloved Novano, a little inkling of that which is to come to the planet.

Did not Novano tell you that she saw the Statue of Liberty with only the torch showing above the waves, and the big skyscrapers of New York tumbling into the waters and the people scrambling around trying to hold onto some floating debris for safety? She saw fires emerging where there had been cities; she saw volcanos rising and erupting which had been dormant for hundreds of years and she saw other things and you have this recorded on tape do you not? So, should you not be willing to accept it as a verification of the prophecies which have been coming forth? I am not going to give you any prophecy this evening for I have given you some already. I do desire to anticipate one of the questions which will be asked me this evening, and I hope that you do not mind for perhaps I can give you more information in my discourse than my simply answering this question.

If you will recall, I gave you some information a long time ago about a meteor coming too close to the Earth which would darken the sun, the moon and the stars. This prophecy is still in effect. I would like to refer you to an article which was channeled through another of our Beloved Channels, whose reliability is beyond question. This has to do with the focal point of a prophecy or the pinpointing of a particular time when a certain event will take place. As I gave you this information, I was looking at a page let us say, in the Cosmic Encyclopedia which predicted this particular effect which would come at approximately that time.

You have been informed, more times than
I could mention, both by my humble self and
your other Masters, that prophecy and events
that predicted events which are destined to
take place upon the planet, in a great many
instances, are modified, or completely changed by the free will of the inhabitants of the
earth. It is not possible, for any prophet, or
any spirit, or any Ascended Master, no matter how highly enlightened or informed or evolv-
ed he may be, to pinpoint an exact prophecy.
This is especially true in these end-times,
when great changes are taking place in the conscious and subconscious minds of the inhabitants of the Earth.

I would suggest that you read the third
and fourth chapters of Jonah, where Jonah, after his episode with the whale, told the people
of Nineveh that they had only forty-two days after which the City would be destroyed. What
did the people tell Jonah? They did not tell
him as many of the people of today are telling
you and the prophets of the present time, "To
_____ with you."

The King and the people of Jonah's day
repented in Sackcloth and Ashes, and the King
declared that all should become contrite in
heart and change their wicked ways immediately.
What happened then? Did God destroy Nineveh?
No, He did not destroy Nineveh -- in 42 days
He spared the city. Why? It was because of
the free will of its inhabitants.

Now, of course, there is a parallel in
this sequel which is occuring in the present
day, and this is the sequel of Jonah's resent-
ment because he had prophesied something that
did not come true. He even chided God for giving him this message and sending him to this
city. So he went out and sat under the shade
of a tree. You know the rest of the story.
Read it.

Yes, a gourd came and sheltered him by day, but then they took away the gourd and he was subjected to the heat of the sun again.

My Beloved Chelas, the same thing may happen again. Yet it is not likely because it would be rather preposterous to suppose that in the short time left for prophecy to be fulfilled, that all the people on earth would repent of their wickedness. So Biblical prophecy and that which is coming forth from reliable channels must be also fulfilled. The Earth must be purged physically, mentally and spiritually and this involves its topography and its inhabitants. I simply wanted to verify the things which have been given to you. Do not say that Master Yogunda was wrong or the prophecy which you have received lately is wrong because there was a different time element involved. The prophecy is true! One of the elements of this prophecy is more profound and in greater detail than the other.

I did not go into extensive detail as to how this darkness would be brought about. I thought that I would explain this to you before you asked me a question about it. However, I would welcome additional questions you desire to know about this situation. Let us go a little further and then I shall bring this discourse to a close. I want to talk about the changes that are coming, the changes that have been in the past, in the present and in the future.

There is no permanency. There is nothing permanent in the Universe and even the galaxies will go into different positions. Do you know that every galaxy in the Universe is travelling at a terrific rate of speed toward a predestined direction? You say, if that is the case, why does it not ever get there? It will <u>never</u> get there because it has all of eternity in

to travel. If you have all of eternity in
which to travel, you will travel throughout
eternity. The direction in which you will
travel will depend, of course, entirely upon
the knowledge and understanding that you have
of the Universal Laws of the Cosmos. The basic
Law of Cause and Effect and all the laws that
stem from it, will be eventually clarified to
you.

You cannot conceive, of course, a small
infinitesimal part of the effect of the Laws
of the Universe because you have a finite mind.
However, your finite mind is directed toward the
Infinite Mind, OM-NI-TOR, thy Creator. The greater rapidity that you can bring your soul into
complete accord and harmony with the Universal
Laws of Life and the Universe, the quicker you
will be able to attain to the Absolute limit
which you can go, but, of course, you never
reach.

My Beloved Ones, I leave you with the admonition that you are to ponder, analyze and
meditate upon all prophecy and all the events
which transpire, not only in your private life,
but in the composite life of the planet you inhabit. Read the signs in the skies, read the
signs in the books, read the signs in your
hearts, conscious and subconscious minds. Put
them altogether and you will have a very composite picture of the past, present and future
of your planet and your own immortal soul.

I believe that I should stop here with that
admonition. I do not wish to bring an anti-
climax to my discourses. I ask you to listen
carefully to all that comes to you and analyze
it, and verify it if possible with all the available facilities at your command, those of the
printed word and your own accumulation of facts
and observations in your conscious and subconscious minds. I will now answer your questions.

Q: We have just received from what we consider a reliable source, or channel, a message
concerning this meteor that is headed for the
Earth and according to the message, dire ef-
fects will result. I won't elaborate upon
this, but we are contemplating putting this
message in printed form and broadcasting it
as much as possible for we find nothing in it
that is not in accordance with the Scriptures.
Would you suggest this be done?

A: My Beloved Chelah, I shall answer your question in two ways. The first part of the question I shall answer with a - Yes. The message is authentic and was received by a channel directly from the Council from which it
was purported to have come. While there are
one or two discrepancies in the message, the
message as a whole is valid and will take
place almost as it was portrayed.

Now as to the next part of your question.
I will leave this to the judgments of your
constituents. I would ask you to analyze and
seek information in regard to publishing this
information.

Let us suppose, for a moment, that you
publish this message, and because of the free
will of the people of earth which is accelera-
ted day by day, the time element which has
been predicted is either extended or modified
in some way. You must determine if you are
ready to take the ridicule and castigation
which may be heaped upon you in the event of
the postponement of the appointed time of this
dire calamity? I am not qualified to say the
time these predictions will come to pass. I
have given this in my discourse. I am sure
that the time I have given you in my own discourse has been extended and you may question
this.

How can the time be extended by a meteor

that is headed for the earth? Well, it is very
simple if you will study the Laws of Nature,
the Laws of the Universe, the magnetic fields
and the vortices which they create. This particular object was slowed in its track by certain conditions which prevailed. Maybe, but it
was not especially the result of the free will
of the inhabitants, but because of the change
in the plans of the Hierarchy. Now I do not know
if this is true or not. As I have told you, I
cannot answer all question. I have only the Cosmic Encyclopedia to consult.

I have given this information now because
the event which I predicted which was to take
place this year will find the condition that
the bases and conditions of the spiritual world
to which these people would be taken, were not
quite ready or prepared, let us say, for this
event at this time. They will be prepared and
they are practically in preparation now, although
there is much work to be done here.

They are giving me the verification that I
am now in contact with the Council of Seven, or
that which is called Solaris and they are in-
structing me to inform you that this event will
take place as scheduled. This is all that I can
give to you about it. My Beloved Ones, it will
be left up to you as what you desire to do about
it. I will not give you any advice because you
are your own inhibitors and arbiters of you own
destinies. However, this is a bona-fide message.

Q: I would appreciate the opportunity, Master
Yogunda to ask you a question. This question is
based on a book which I have in my hand, issued
by William Ferguson who claims to be the Voice
of Truth. He has issued a book about the Book
of Revelations which is supposed to be a revelation by the Revelator, Himself. He claims to
be the Revelator, and that he is the incarnation
of John, the Revelator. His claims are based
on the seventh verse in the Tenth Chapter, and

the tenth verse of the Eleventh Chapter, in
the days of the Voice of the Seventh Angel,
and also this command was given to John
that he must prophesy again before many
peoples, and nations, and tongues and kings.
He says in the following chapter the above
instructions are fulfilled by the Revelator,
who, today, is known as William Ferguson, the
Voice of Truth.

Now, I have my suspicion of the authenticity of this and would appreciate it if
you could repudiate or confirm this for us.

A: My Beloved Chelah, thank you very much
for asking this question. I will be very
happy to clarify it for you. Again I say
that I cannot answer a question by a 'yes'
or a 'no'. This is one of those questions.
However, I will give you a full explanation
and a clarification of it.

Let us go back to some of my former discourses and some of those which have been
given to you by our Beloved Rama and by Mother Mary. This is in regard to many of these
Beloved Channels who bring forth spiritual
truth and prophesy which is necessary to be
imparted to the minds of the people.

Before I answer your question, I will
refer to one whom I have previously mention-
ed, who claims to be the incarnated Mother
Mary. Now if I were to come right out and
say these are not the incarnated entities
whom they claim to be, then I would be doing
a disservice for them and for you. Let me
explain.

These individuals, and I will include
several, and two especially of whom I have
given you information in the past are overshadowed by the Arch Angel or Chohan, or Spirit.
In this particular case, this Beloved Soul,

Brother Ferguson, is completely overshadowed
by John, the Revelator. The overshadowing
is in such a manner or degree of vibration
that he has assumed he is the reincarnated,
John, the Revelator. To him, this is perfectly real and has even been given information
in this regard that he is St. John, the Revelator.

Does it make any difference whether he is
or not? However, it does make a difference to
you and others who read the book for if he is
not St. John, the Revelator, then, of course,
the book starts with a lie, does it not? The
book does contain not only prophecy, but highly spiritual truths which corroborates with
all Spiritual Truth, which has been brought
forth. The contents of the book is almost
perfect. However, the author is one with the
Beloved Revelator. He is a Revelator for he
has revealed in this little book, pertinent
information for these last days.

In another case, Mother Mary has overshadowed a certain individual to such an extent that she actually believes that she is
the Beloved Mother Mary. Mother Mary has also verified this for you, has she not?

There are many who claim at the present
time to have had a specific incarnation, but
they are not what you would call valid state-
ments, but by the fact if they are overshadowed,
it is very close to the truth.
I will try to give you a discourse on the
subject of "Overshadowing" and the difference
between overshadowing and actual reincarnation.
There is quite a difference, yet it has many
of the same characteristics. Does that satis-
fy you, My Beloved Brother?

Q: Yes, thank you, it is very enlightening.

Q: Master Yogunda, this is a question from a
reader. Who was the Guardian Angel or Arch-

Angel who was over the barn announcing the
birth of Jesus to the nearby Shepherds and who
led the Wise Men to the Baby Jesus? I was told
some years ago that this Guardian Angel had
charge over Jesus and that she was a very beautiful Angel. This was told to me by an Initiate.

A: Well, My Beloved Ones, and My Beloved Reader, again I must answer that question in a rather indirect way. There were about several thousand Angels or Announcers and the one that was
seen at that particular time was the Arch-Angel,
Gabriel. By His side was His feminine counter-
part, who was more in evidence to those present
than the Arch Angel himself for he was in the
background. As you know, the Arch Angel Gabriel has been designated as the Announcer, or the
the One who "blows the horn." So He was blowing his horn very loudly, and his companion
was also giving the messsage at the same time.
There were many who heard the music of Gabriel's
Host at that particular time. Therefore, there
was not one specific angel, but there were thousands of Guardian Angels. There were one or
two who were visible above and over the rest
of them,

        I hope this will answer the question for
our reader. Of course, it does not make much
difference who he was or what his name was,
except that it is nice to know these things.

Q: May I ask   a question concerning the Flying Saucers that were over our coastal City
recently? You told us there was a certain pois-
on that came from the ocean. Can you tell us
what this element was, and what caused it?

A: Yes, this was part of the atomic explosion
which was detonated in France and was also ac-
centuated by another vortex which had formed
some 800 miles off the Coast of the United
States in the Pacific Ocean. It was not something especially deadly, but it had combined

with the already detrimental tests which had occured at that particular point.

Q: Well we have enjoyed your answers and that is all the questions for tonight.

A: I enjoy answering the questions for you for I know you are always anxious to find some particular phase of the Universal Laws which you would like explained. It is something that concerns you, but does not particularly bother you.

Those within the sound of my voice have come here faithfully and are not the type to be bothered. You are the type who are seeking continually information, physical, mental and spiritual which will help you to live a fuller and better life. For this, I commend you.

No I shall commend your body, mind and spirit to the Father above Who is the Author and Finisher of our faith, all of our faith, every faith, everything we have.

I now bless you and bid you Godspeed and a blessed Good night. This is Master Yogunda, speaking.

So many Gods, so many creeds,
So many paths that wind and wind,
When just the art of being kind
Is all the sad world needs.

-- Ella Wheeler Wilcox

MASTER YOGUNDA

Discourse # 129   Nov. 10, 1966

GGGGG REETINGS AND SALUTATIONS, Beloved Chelahs
G GG of Light. Dear friends all; all of you
GGGGG are Chelahs and everyone who enters this
room I regard as a Chelah.

      Of course, there is little difference be-
tween a Chelah and a student. A Chelah is one
who has stepped upon the path of progression
and is also a student. A student may be a student in name only and will not continue nor
absorb the studies they have started. There
is a difference between a Chelah and a student.
I always welcome you as Chelahs, regardless of
whether your physical presence has been mani-
fested here or not.

      I welcome you all as I always do and I
know that you welcome me, or else you would
not come, and I would not be able to project
to you any of these teachings and information
which comes from my humble presence.

      Now, I do not have any particular intro-
duction so I shall go immediately into my discourse and it will be continuation of a question which was asked some time ago. I did not
answer it for you fully because I wanted to
give you more information about it and there
were several interpretations which may be placed
upon it and I will dwell upon it now.

      The subject of my discourse is: The Dwel-
ler on The Threshold. The Dweller on the Threshold is a scriptural reference and one that has
been interpreted in many different ways. Tonight,
I shall give you three interpretations or rather I will bring forth my discourse in a parable
as usual so you will understand exactly what
I am speaking about when I elucidate upon the
Dweller on the Threshold.

Now, My Beloved Ones, all of you in the
physical, at the moment are dwellers on the
threshold. I am speaking now not only to those
within the sound of my voice but those who
study to be approved by the Masters and OM-
NI-TOR, Thy Creator. If you are studying and
looking out upon a world of confusion and chaos,
you are dwellers upon the threshold. You are
beckoning to those are   without. I will
compare this now to the threshold of a beautiful room or building which is filled with
Light, the Light of the Universe, the Christ
Light. You are standing on this threshold
with outstretched arms. Most of you are beckoning those who are passing by, but who pay
no attention perhaps to your beckoning or the
open door they are passing at the moment. There
are thousands and thousands of them who do not
recognize a dweller on the threshold. They do
not recognize there is a room or a condition of
Light and Love to which they may go without in-
terference, without effort, to partake of the
Essence within that room of Light and Love.

So continue, my beloved ones, to dwell upon
the threshold. There is also a simile here for
if you withdraw within this room, and shut the
door, you will, of course, be bathed in the
great Christ Light and the Light of the Universe.

You will be partaking of this only in your
own restricted way for as you stand upon the
threshold, you will not only be able to receive
this Light and bathe yourself in it, but you
will be able to reflect it to all those without who are attracted to you and they will be
able to bathe themselves, their minds, their
bodies and their Spirits in that Light. You
may, by some word or deed, be able to invite .
them to the great Assembly of God, the great
Assembly of Light where you, yourselves, have
been experiencing the great ecstasy of these
experiences.

It is not possible for you to go outside
of the threshold among those friends of yours,
and shut the door behind you because then you
will be dwelling in the same condition of darkness in which they are in. So you must always
keep the door open and dwell upon the threshold of Light and Love. Eventually, many of
them will be attracted to your Light upon the
threshold.

Now I shall give you another metaphor
about those who are dwelling upon the threshold. They are not in physical bodies. They are
the Great Masters and those who have gone long
before to the spiritual realms, and those great
souls who are from other dimensions and planets
in the Universe. They are dwelling upon the
threshold of Light and beckoning to you, proclaiming with a trumpet sound, the glories of
the Universe and the glories that may be yours
by simply coming to the Assembly of Light and
finding your place within its confines. These
are those whom may be termed, "The Invisible
Helpers." There have been several books written about the invisible helpers.

There are countless millions of them in
the Universe at large and you have received
messages from many of them. Lately you have
received the ultimate, let me say, of this
Light which you will be required to emanate
to the world as you, in physical form, are
dwelling upon the threshold. This has been
deeded to you from other dwellers upon the
threshold who have much less dense bodies than
yourselves. They may be termed 'ephemeral' or
"etheric' as the case may be.

You are now working together with all
other dwellers upon the threshold and you are
One together. You must not be separated, and
you cannot be separated in these last days
of the configuration of the present inhabitants of the Planet Earth. I use the word

because the condition, as you well know, of the
inhabitants of your planet and its geographical
contour will be very rapidly changed in the next
two or three years of time. Perhaps, I should
dwell upon this element also, but I will not
go into it as I feel you have some questions in
this regard which I may be able to answer for
you at the end of my discourse.

There is a third classification of the
Dwellers upon the Threshold. This is not a negative aspect in any way, but you may consider
it so. This will give you a greater responsibility and a greater insight into the respon-
sbilities that are transferred upon you. Now
there are many, many who are dwelling upon the
threshold and are looking in. You have been
looking out and those from the more etheric
planes have also been looking out and down upon you. These many thoasands of others who
are looking in are now _upon_ the threshold. They
have been attracted to the light and have knowledge of their own life, their past, present
and future and they are pondering whether or
not to enter this great effusion of Light or
whether it will blind them, or whether it will
be too much form them to encounter at this particular time. They are hesitating upon the
threshold and are looking in.

It is your responsibility to lower Light
for them a little so they may understand or
comprehend a little better what lies ahead,
for sometimes those who are suddenly attracted
 to this Light and Love, this Universal Light
 and Love, are blinded and they stumble and
fall across the threshold, and do not enter
the fullness of Light

You must take them by the hand and gently
lead them for they cannot go alone into the fullness of this Light and Love. Therefore, you have
a double responsibility of emanating Light upon the threshold, and also the responsibility

32-

of bringing those who are upon the threshold
who have been attracted by your Light to an
understadable knowledge of that which lies
ahead.

So that, My Beloved Chelahs of Light,
is the meaning of the Dweller on the Threshold. Perhaps, it is not the same as the scriptural reference has been interpreted. Previously I gave you a very superficial interpretation because I wanted to dwell upon it
more fully at a future time. So now I have
given you a resume, and I hope, a little better understanding of the Dweller upon the
Threshold and what it entails and the respon-
sibilities that rest upon you as Chelahs of
Light as you dwell upon the threshold and look
about you upon a confused and chaotic world.

So, My Beloved Ones, I shall close my
discourse and shall proceed to answer your
questions for I fell that you have a number
of them that may shed a little more light upon the Threshold and a little more Light upon
those who are grasping for additional Light,
and even for you, that you may understand a
little more about the manifestations that are
coming to your planet in a very short time.

God bless you, each and every one. I
will now answer your questions for you.

Q: Master Yogunda, in reading the book, "The
Invisible Helpers, it also gives another interpretation of the Dweller on the Threshold,
and calls it the Sin Body that builds which
is the Dweller on the Threshold?

A: This is another interpretation and is actually the scriptural interpretation. Of course,
it is symbolical and the "Dweller" may go
either way. The symbology of that is, it
may go either into the Light or out into the
darkness as the Chelah desires.

Q: I have some questions on a prophecy that
came to us because people are asking me about
them. Will you explain: Why no death? Will
it be because the Earth will be placed in
the fourth dimension after the three days of
darkness?

A: **No,** My Beloved Chelah, that is not correct.
First of all, the message did not say there
would be no death. It said these people could
not die, or would not die to relieve their pain
and suffering, although they wanted to die. It
did not say, they would <u>never</u> die. After the
earth is restored to a somewhat normal condition and the holocaust is over and has expend-
ed its fury, then these people will be in two
classifications.

I will give you this information as I
have been studying it myself since it was projected to you, and, of course, I've known something about it before but did not want to elaborate upon it before.

I do want to briefly clarify this subject
for you. The Earth will not pass through the
4th dimension. This is not the 4th dimension.
The word, 'dimensions' is not the proper word,
although we will use it here. The 4th dimension is the Spirit World. It is a world of
ethereal substance -- that is the 4th dimension. When you speak of the 4th dimension,
this is the realm to which you go in your as-
tral travels. The Earth will not be in the
4th dimension even after the axis has settled
and will be in its new orbit. It will be the
same Earth as before, but will be in a new
orbit and will have an entirely different configuration in the Solar System. It will be
the same Earth as before, except, of course,
you would not recognize it if you were there
before and you had suddenly come back again.
The Earth will pass through a complete change
and purging.

Those who are taken away and are appointed to be returned as inhabitants and teachers, as well as Chelahs of Light for the rehabilitation of the New Earth, will be brought back, and it will be your responsibility, if you are one of these, to teach those who are left who have gone through the tribulations. Does not your Scripture tell you about the tribulations? This is the tribulation. Therefore, it will be left to you to try to instruct them. Many of them will be reformed and rejuvenated into a higher frequency of essence. Many of them will remain and will not be reformed or saved as you might term it. These people will eventually die in a certain length of time because you will not want these people upon the earth to encumber it with their evil forces, would you? Therefore, this will be done in a Divine, orderly manner, at the end. No, the Earth will not go into the 4th dimension, and these people will see death just as any other, but they will not see it because they want to see it. That will be their punishment if you want to call it punishment. Of course, punishment is something you bring upon yourself. God does not punish any one in the Universe. You punish yourselves, is that clear?

Q: Will you explain the insect hordes. Do they come from Icarus?

A: No, these giant insects, some of them, will emerge from the inner earth as the new openings will be made. If you will remember the message which tells of the new openings in the earth. Some will come from the inner earth and some will come from, or be transported from a planet which will come closer to your earth which is not inhabited.

No, these will not persist for any length of time. They will come, and then they will go. This message should have given you this information, but, of course, the message was long and could not give you every detail of

Dictated by Jesus of Nazareth.   Channel R.M.Balz,1936—Novato blvd.
Novato,Calif.

VANITY FAIR.

When springtime comes over the hill, Blowing blowing the
When summer comes over the hill, Blowing blowing the
When autumn comes over the hill, Blowing blowing the

When winter comes over the hill, B lowing blowing the

gentle wind Nature takes off her mantle of snow so you can
balmy breeze Nature puts on a permanent wave in fields of
frosty wind The frost tickle nature on the nose and make her

icy wind Nature puts on a mantle of snow and ici —

see her green dress you,
wheat and fields of hay,
blush all red and yellow,

I know, When springtime blows the gentle wind Na-
When summer blows the balmy breeze Na-
When autumn blows the frosty wind, Na-

-cles upon her brow, When winter blows the icy wind Na

C⁷

F

-ture hangs up the pussy willows, When springtime blows the gentle
-ture hides blue buttons in the hay, When summer blows the balmy
-ture all her flowers let go, When autumn blows the frosty

- ture put white slippers on her toes, When winter blows the icy

F

wind, Nature paints the butter cups yellow.
breeze, Nature hides red poppies in the hay.
wind, The leaves turn crimson red and yellow.
wind, Nature turns white wherever she goes.

this information.

This will be temporary, and they will not
molest you after the tribulation and when you
are brought back the earth will be re-populated.

Those who will be saved will not be the
only inhabitants upon the earth. Others will
be brought here from a higher dimension and
some will be brought from other planets, some
from Venus and some from outside of your Galaxy.
As you have been promised by both the Scriptures and your Space People, you will have a
Paradise. Of what will this Paradise consist?
You would not have anything evil or anything
negative in this Paradise, would you? Therefore this will be something fiar beyond your
comprehension at the present time. This is
all that I can give you now.

Q: What about the people in the Inner Earth?
Will they be affected too?

A: Yes, they will. Some of them will emerge
and come to the surface, and some will go into
the inner earth.   There will be an exchange
from these two areas. The inner earth has not
been accepted except in a very limited manner
until now. A few of the spacecraft which you
see in your skies have come from the inner
earth. They are for reconnaissance and friendly purposes. However, there are very few of
them which have an evil intent as I have told
you. The Space People have told you that these
ones have been practically cleared from your
skies and will not bother you. They will be
entirely cleared away during the holocaust.

Q: Master Yogunda, I have a personal interest
in the Hawaiian Islands. Will you please give
me a little background on this and also the
beautiful people that inhabit those Islands.

A: Yes, My Beloved Chelah. These people are
descendants in a remote way from the Mayans,

the inhabitants of Central America and part of
Mexico. They have a very highly developed
spiritual nature and have great rapport with
the Nature Devas. They are very friendly in
nature, in fact, the most friendly on the face
of the Earth at the present time. If you make
a friendly gesture toward them, there is not
one stone which they will leave unturned to ac-
comodate you and please you. If you cross them
they can be just the opposite, and they can be
potent enemies. Very few are in this category.

The Hawaiin Islands are a remnant of one
of the submerged constinents the same as Japan
is a remnant of the great continent of Pan.
Jap -- J-A-P means remnant, a remnant of Pan.

The Hawaiin Islands are a remnant. This is
one reason they are so highly developed and
friendly. There is much history behind this
Island and its people which I cannot now give
you.

You, My Beloved Chelah, will have a wonderful experience there which you do not now
anticipate. You will learn something there
that will prove to be of great benefit to you.
This is not just a pleasure trip that you are
taking. You will be very pleased with what you
will observe on this particular trip you are
going to take.

(The following question was asked by Florence
Karsleigh whose obituary is found in this issue. Master Yogunda was somewhat reluctant
to answer it, but she insisted (a characteris-
tic of this recent incarnation and others.),
so here is the answer. The visitors referred
to were her two daughters who had passed over
to the Spiritual Realm several years ago.)

Q: My question is more of a personal nature,
but I think everyone will be interested. I
would like to know the meaning of the Light
that penetrated my room and also about the

visitors who visited me four times in one night?

A: My Beloved Chelah, are you sure you desire an interpretation of that vision? I will give you an interpretation in one or two sentences and that is all I can give.

It was a very real vision and, of course, it was entirely symbolical. The Light was the Light of the Christ or the Heavenly Light that was projected by your visitors. The relatives were your daughters. I believe that is correct? They were there to give you a message, but did not give one particular message at that time. All of this is in preparation of a "journey" that you are to take in a very SHORT TIME. This is all that I can give you about this vision today, my Beloved Chelah.

Q: What is the meaning of the bed or cot that he was carrying? (A bier, perhaps? Ed.)

A: It was symbolical only of the "journey".

Q: Is there such a thing as a "Lost Soul?"

A: Ha! Ha! -- such a thing as a Lost Soul! Yes, there are many lost souls, but we perhaps should put the word "lost" in quotation marks. What do we mean by a "Lost Soul?" Do you mean temporarily or permanently lost? If you mean permanently lost, the answer is no. If you mean temporarily lost, the answer is yes.

Now it may seem that I am speaking in riddles. There are many souls who are lost in the chaos and confusion of their environment. They may be lost in the physical body or they may be lost in the spiritual body, but they are certainly not lost forever.

The Scripture has been misinterpreted and as our Beloved Sananda has told you many times it has been manipulated to suit the interest of the Priesthood, especially of a certain

dominant domination. You know what I am speaking about. There is no such thing as a lost
soul. There are many souls that are temporarily lost, but will be regained eventually.

Now I will go back to a rather hazy
statement:There are certain conditions under
which a soul, after a certain period of time,
is dissolved. You have been told this by two
or three of the Masters who have stated that
if a soul does not progress in a certain length
of time it goes back to a primordial condition.
If. there is no hope that this soul will ever
progress then the soul, itself is dissolved and
a new soul is born from that which remains of
the old soul. This is a very vague statement
which I cannot amplify at this time.

There is, however, nothing really lost in
the Universe. The soul that is'lost' is not
lost, for a new soul is formed from the remain-
der of the one that was dissolved.

Your Scripture says that man was made from
the dust of the earth. This is another vague
statement. What is the dust of the earth, and
how was man made from the dust of the earth? I
could spend several hours upon this subject,
but I will not.

The dust of the Earth is the essence of
Creation. The Earth was created, and the Universe was created, and therefore, man was created. In order to give some kind of explanation
of how man was created, then it was simply said,
that he was created from the dust of the earth.

Q: You spoke about my going on a long journey,
can you tell me more about this journey?

(Florence's insistence. She returned to hospital
five days before death. -- Ed.).

A: No, My Beloved Chelah, I will leave it there.
You will understand it later.

(Continued page 67)

Eastport Plaza   Nov. 13, 1966

L
E   IGHT AND BLESSINGS be unto thee! My
E   Beloved Ones, let thy Light shine for-
ELLLL ever and forever as you have prayed. I
come to you this afternoon in that Love and
Light to enable you to bring forth a better ef-
fulgence of this Light in all that you say and
do.

    I AM SANANDA, your Wayshower. I do not pre-
fer the designation of Cosmic Host for I will
come to you as your Cosmic Wayshower. This does
not mean that I will not come from time to time
to bring other Masters, Arch Angels and even
Elohim who will speak to you of things of Heav-
en and Earth. I will, as opportunity presents,
bring these Blessed Ones to you.

    This afternoon, I desire to address you as
One whose heart and soul is in essence always
with you and among you. Although I have the
designation of your Teacher in this New Age
Dispensation, I AM only a Cosmic Emissary of
the teachings and the knowledge that you should
know and absorb at this time. So, My Beloved
ONes, it gives me great joy that I can come
to you, and I will each time the opportunity
presents itself.

    I desire to tell you briefly the reason
why I replaced your Beloved Novano, and perhaps, it would be well that I answered one of
the questions that has been upon your minds.
The question is: If our Sister of Light is going to reincarnate on the Earth Plane and the
time is so short, why is it necessary? This is
one of the mysteries of the Cosmos and will not
be a mystery to you, as I will explain it.

    I have so much that I desire to tell you
this afternoon that I cannot finish it in the
allotted time. In future visits with you, many

of the things our Beloved Master Yogunda has given you, I will clarify and amplify for you. Now to answer this question.

First of all, I desire to corroborate or evaluate the message which you have received in regard to the vast, extensive, far-reaching changes which are coming to earth and its inhabitants. Of course, there are many questions in your minds, but let me tell you briefly there will be thousands and thousands of children lifted from the earth plane before and during the time of the catastrophe. This will include the Babes-in-Arms to the Teen-Agers, and those who have been reincarnated for a very specific purpose to carry on the work.After the Cosmic Dust has settled and the Cosmic Masters have proclaimed a holiday, so to speak, some of the Masters will descend in person (not my humble self for awhile), but many of the Masters will descend to be among you and they will be accompanied by those thousands who will return to the Earth's surface to rehabilitate it.

Of course, our Beloved Novano will be among them. Why did she not wait until the time was over? Well, that would not be in the Divine Plan for she would not be prepared at that time, if the years rolled by, for she has a specific work to do as a male incarnate in the New and Wondrous New Age that is yet to come to the Planet Earth.

I hope this will answer the question that has been in your minds, about the children who have been incarnated or who are here at the present time. Children will continue to incarnate and those who are in the womb at that time will also be protected if they are to come forth as incarnate beings of Light, into the greater effulgence of the New Age.

* * * * *

MASTER YOGUNDA

Discourse # 130   Nov. 16, 1966

GGGGG
G   REETINGS AND SALUTATIONS, Beloved Ones
G   GG   of Light. Master Younda speaking. I
GGGGG   AM indeed happy this evening that I
can come again to you in this manner and
through this Channel. I hope that this will
be a worth-while visit which we shall have
together.

     I wish to emphasize that these are vis-
its and that I AM not in any sense of the word,
a superior being over, above and beyond you,
My Beloved Chelas, except that I have traversed
the path of Light to a point of Light where-
in I can shed that Light and to give it to a
darkened world through human channels. I will
use the plural for I have now spoken through
five different channels. I wish to state
and I hope that you will not get an egoistic
feeling about this, but our Beloved Channel
and your Organization is my <u>primary</u> <u>love,</u>
and the ones to whom I have assigned my efforts and to whom I felt I could bring in
volume and effulgence, these messages and
discourses which would go to all humanity
over all the earth, and I have been completely justified in my assumption.

.   I desire at this time to commend you and
thank you all who have had any part in the
dissemination of these messages and for your
love and persistence and also your untiring
efforts in this work. Not only do I thank
our Beloved Channel, but I thank all of you
for if it were not for you, it would be possible perhaps, but not as effective as the
Spiritual Hierarchy has decreed as it should
be. I wish also to commend you in my preface
this evening which will be quite lengthy.

- 42

I will be speaking to you about giving
the message of "evil" about which I desire to
commend you for your courage in this respect.
The "Icarus" message I have designated as 90%
correct and it took a considerable amount of
courage to bring this to the attention of the
public in the volume which you have done.
This volume has only started and you will be
able to bring this to the attention of many
thousands in the very near future. They will
be stimulated and encouraged to have the information necessary to act upon, if they are
to receive the approval of the Spiritual Hierarchy and the Ascended Masters.

Of course, many thousands will scoff at
the prediction and will turn away just as they
did in the days of Noah. You cannot help this
situation and are not responsible for them,
but you are responsible for those to whom you
do not give this information. I do not mean
that you can always designate exactly to whom
you should send this material, but you will
be able to send it to hundreds who will assimi-
late it -- and believe it -- and make prepara-
tions for these forthcoming events which will
take place upon the earth.

There has arisen, perhaps, a question
in your mind which I will clarify at this
time. If this message is true, why did I not
give you this information before, rather than
wait for it to come from an outside source? I
will explain that to you briefly and I hope
you will understand it. There is a Divine Plan
for each individual and for each group of individuals and for the earth, itself.

I could have given you this information
in almost the same language for I knew it was
coming. I could not have given it to you in
as great a detail perhaps as it was given, but
I could have given you a synopsis at least.

Suppose that I had given this message. It would not have been as effective and would not have reached as many people as it did and will reach, if I had brought it. You have published this material, not in your magazine, but extra copies so that it might reach many thousands of people. You would have felt rather obligated to put this message, if I had given it to you, in your magazine, as you do the rest of my messages. This wonderful little publication you have named, or rather the Hierarchy has named, "The Voice of Universarius."

So, this was all arranged in this way. You will have other messages which I will not give you. The fact that I have verified its authenticity will also add to its prestige as it goes out in future editions. Now I hope that you will understand why I did not give you this message. Perhaps I should reiterate that all the Spiritual Hierarchy work in harmony together. There is no jealousy, no discrimination, recrimination or negation between any of those who work for the evolvement and the emancipation of the Planet Earth.

This is not the case, of course, on your planet, for just the opposite is true. It grieves us no end that even those groups who are classified as Channels of Light, and those who are trying to spread the Light of the New Age have a certain amount of jealousy or recrimination among themselves just as the Orthodox Churches have had, and still have, throughout the centuries. This must be eliminated. As we see it, it cannot be aCHIEVED in the immediate future. Each must be autonomous in their own right and they must give out what is given to them, fearlessly and without leaning upon any other group or channel. Of course, you will recognize in reading the messages of other channels, all material is not alike; it has much variation. This is as it should be. If the material were all alike, it would be monotonous and it would not serve the purpose for which it was designed. Therefore, all is in harmony and rhythm and follows a Divine Plan.

I AM giving you one phase of instruction for your evolvement through our Beloved Channel. Others of the Hierarchy including myself, are giving another phase of instruction through other channels, most of which is published. However, there are many good messages which should go out to the world, but does not go any further than the little circumscribed group in which they are received. Of course, the group which receives them, expands in their consciousness and it is for their edification that they tell others about it and eventually their work and teachings will expand outside of their small limits.

This is a longer introduction than I had intended to give you, but I would be amiss if I did not include a hearty welcome for those who have come to partake of this service and listen to my humble self for the first time. This includes others also who have come spasmodically. I also welcome them to this session, and I hope that it will be a, more or less, regular practice with them, and that we can visit together more often and under more auspicious circumstances.

All of you are Chelahs of Light, whether you are new, or whether you have been here for many, many times before. You are Chelahs because you are desirous of learning more about the hidden meaning of life, more about yourselves, more about those individuals and groups about you. So if you have a desire to learn about something, it is commendable.

Oh, My Beloved Ones, it saddens my heart many, many times when I look upon your world and see the thousands and millions of souls who have no desire or interest in learning more than their physical eyes can see, what their physical ears can hear. What a sad state for the Creation the Heavenly Father has so perfectly created in the Planet Earth as a place of evolvement for mankind.

I see and feel these things very intensely and it makes me redouble my effort to bring you many of the things which all of the inhabitants of the earth should know more about.

Again I wish to commend you and thank you for this will never cease with me, but I do not want to dwell upon it too long.

This is my introduction. Sometimes it is short and sometimes it is long. It depends upon how I feel and how you feel and how the vibration is in the room. I wish to commend you for a very high frequency vibration this evening. Now I have decided that I would sit at the head and shoulders of our Channel this evening to channel this message to you. Some may be able to see me, but if you do not, it is well. Some other time perhaps you will be able to see me or perceive me in your thoughts.

I have chosen a subject upon which I will dwell briefly after that lengthy introduction. My subject tonight is "THE PLOW AND THE HARROW." Well, I am not addressing farmers that I know of, yet, as always, I tell you, these things are symbols in parables and metaphors, that you may understand, just as our Beloved Jesus (Sananda) told his disciples that they might understand him. I hope that you may be able to recall and retain some of the things which I have told you so that it might sink into your consciousness. I do not expect you to recall all of it, for that would be an extraordinary task. However, for some, it would

be an ordinary task. I know there are some who
come here, who can remember practically everything that I say. Now back to my subject.

"The Plow and the Harrow." Why does the
farmer use the plow and the harrow to turn
over the soil after a crop has been harvested
or even on fallow ground or ground thatihas not
been put to use before?

I am going to use symbology this evening
for the ground must be prepared and a seed bed
must be prepared for a new crop, after the old
one has been harvested.

Now many of you who have received this
very important message (The message on Icarus),
are wondering why these things are necessary
to happen to earth. Why cannot it be renovated
and those seeds sown upon the top soil without all the changes which are coming? It is
for the same reason that the farmer prepares
his ground. There must be a complete recon-
struction of the ground before any seed will
sprout. You cannot sow the seed on top of
the ground and expect it to take root, can you?
Therefore, you cannot expect a new Heaven and
Earth constructed from an old Heaven and Earth,
if it is not plowed and harrowed, so to speak.
This is symbolical of the changes coming to
the earth. You must have prepared a fallow
seed bed in which to plant the seeds of the
New Age for those souls who will inhabit the
earth after it has settled down from its con-
vulsions and cataclysms or whatever you wish
to call them.

Now there is another symbology that I
would like to bring you. After the seed is
planted, it will take some time to grow. There
have been some erroneous ideas regarding the
New Age in that it is coming suddenly. It
will grow from the remains which have been
left intact when the earth has found its place
in the Solar System.

This is not a sudden change, although the change itself will come suddenly. There will be a steady growth, but not as slow as the 6th Dispensation or the previous ones which have come and gone on the earth since its creation. There will be a very rapid growth and a rapid change and the seed will come forth and bring fruit and desires of the Spirit from the new soil of the New Age which will be placed upon the Planet Earth in the next few years.

I am glad that our Channel read to you from the Psalms which will allay your fears in regard to that which is coming. You, My Beloved Chelans have nothing to fear. Some of you, of course, will be taken without notice and :without any of your possessions. There is a word of caution that I would like to bring you now. I will bring to you, subsequently, my analysis of this which is not yet complete for it must be analyzed thoroughly as we go along.You must.ndt retain in your memory any of the desires of the flesh or a desire to hold on to your possessions. When you return from your pleasant journey into space from some planet, VEnus, perhaps, which is prepared to give you the schooling while you are there, you will be supplied with all the necessities of life and all those things necessary to rehabilitate the New Earth. The New Earth shall blossom an.d be as velvet under your feet.

There will be in the minds of thousands, perhaps, who will contemplate upon the situation -- "What will become of my possessions?" "What will become of my house?" "What will become of this or that possession?"

You have them now, of course, for your comfort and livelihood. You should keep them as long as it is feasible, but when the time comes to leave them, have no regrets about

- 48

leaving them, for they will be returned to you
a hundred-fold, not as they are now, but in
a more ethereal and spiritual degree, although
they shall yet be physical.

It is far beyond your comprehension at
this moment just what will take place upon the
New Earth when it is brought into the fullness
of its manifestation where it takes its right-
ful place in the new alignment of the Solar
System.

This is all that I can bring you tonight.
I shall bring you more on this subject as we
progress in our analysis of these coming events
which will take place.

Before I go into the question and answer
period, I would like to make remark about your
Beloved Tom who is away. He is now at a party
and he is having a very pleasant time He can
verify this when he returns. You can ask him
when he returns what he was doing on Wednesday
night. Now, I will answer your question, Beloved Chelahs.

Q: Master Yogunda, I want to ask you what will
happen to the monetary system in the New Earth?

A: Of course, all systems, monetary, or other-
wise will be dissolved during the events which
will transpire during the time the planet goes
through the changes and evolution. The new system which will emerge will not be called the
monetary system. Money assets will not be used
as a medium of exchange. I cannot give you the
details of this new system, but will have to
be planned by those who return. There will be
no monetary system or such medium of exchange
as we now have on earth. Does that answer your
question?

Do not hesitate, My Beloved Chelahs, if
you have a question for I am always happy to
answer them for you. As I told you, I will
look into my Cosmic Encyclopedia if I do not

find the answer there, I will not hesitate to
tell you and will look it up for you next time.
If I cannot find it, I will also let you know.
I am not infallible and I am not Infinite as
I AM only a Master upon the Fifth Spiritual
Plane who has access to this Cosmic Encyclo-
pedia which will answer most of your ques-
tions

Q: I have been reading about the Life of Jesus
in the book called Urantia. There seems to be
some discrepancy between the Aquarian Gospel
of Jesus Christ by Levi and Urantia. Which
one is right, or are they both right in a sense?
Is one spiritual and one material?

A: You are correct, My Beloved Chelah. There
are a few discrepancies. As I have told you before, there are none of the Holy Books which
are 100% percent correct. The only discrepancy
between these two books is about the travels
of Jesus, and this you may have discerned. He
was at some time in the occult schools, both
in Tibet and Palestine and Egypt also. There
is very little discrepancy, except one is more
complete than the other.

The Book of Urantia is perhaps the most
complete account, and the most accurate in regard to the events in the Life of Jesus that
has come to the Earth Plane at this time.

Q: I had a feeling that probably in the Aquarian Gospel where it tells of his travels and
attending these various schools, that He went
there spiritually, instead of in the physical.
Am I right?

A: That is correct. Yes.

Q: Master Yogunda, I have had several people
ask me about this lecturer who saw the Flying
Saucers from Mars. They have asked me what
did he say about birth, death, and the life-
span and I could not answer as I do not know,

because he did not mention it. I thought maybe you could give me some information about
the life on the Planet Mars?

A: I will tell you briefly that all the planets
are a great deal alike which will include Mars
and Venus. There is little difference between
Mars and Venus. However, the inhabitants of
Mars are somewhat taller than those of Venus
and they are somewhat denser. Now, if you, in
your physical body were to visit Venus, you
would not be able to see any of the people
there. This is the reason why the pictures
of Venus, and even the moon, show no life upon
the Planet. However, they are just as real
and as solid as you are, yet they are in an entirely different vibration -- a higher vibration.

The method of birth and so-called death
upon Venus is entirely different and takes
place upon the etheric plane. Mars is like the
earth, but somewhat different. The average
length of life upon Mars is 250 years. The life
span on Venus is very indefinite. They live as
long as their life is useful. They can trans-
cend to a life of higher vibration or higher
realm. Just as we have Heaven and Earth, they
have their higher realms on all of the other
planets. Just as many have done before, I did
not have to die and my death was not premature.
I simply laid it down when I was ready to go
into a higher vibration

Birth upon the Planet Mars is about the
same as upon the Earth, except that it is advanced scientifically. There is no pain, of
course. Birth upon Mars is regulated by the
desires of the incoming entities and their
parents. There is complete cooperation between
the reimbodiment of the entity upon Mars and the
parents of the entity. Of course, this is not
the case now upon the Earth Plane.

There are many other things I could tell
you but I do not have the time. I promise I
will give you more information in the future
and I may delegate this to one of the higher
beings who will bring one of the teachers
to tell you more about it.. I will make this
a promise. I will try to bring you someone
from these various realms who can give you a
more comprehensive and detailed description
of life upon these planets than I can give
you from this vantage point. Does that answer your question?

Tonight I thank you for your presence,
for your vibration and for everything that
you have brought, not only to me, but yourselves as well. Anything that you bring with
you, whether it is your higher consciousness
or your vibration is appreciated by all of
the Spiritual Hierarchy.

They are standing by, listening atten-
tively to the discourses which I give to you.
They listen to the discourses which are given
by the Ascended Masters and they are monitored.
Did you know that everything upon the Earth
Plane is monitored? Sometimes, we have conferences such as you have upon the Earth Plane
where we discuss what might be said, or what
should be left out by our Mentors and Instruc-
tors. There is no end to instruction in the
Etheric Realm. Again, there is no end to instructions on the Earth Plane. As above, so
below, as the saying goes.

I will now close my discourse and I thank
you for your questions and for your attention..

Good night and God bless you. This is
Master Yogunda speaking.

* * * * *

MASTER YOGUNDA

Discourse #131   Nov. 23, 1966

PPPP
PPPP P EACE, PEACE, be unto thee.;I bring you
P   blessings and glory and all the Light
P   and Love of the Universal Fatherhood
and Brotherhood of Man as they are emanated
from all parts of the Universe to the Planet
Earth at this time. I bring you all the bles-
sings that I can hold within my grasp.

I AM Master Yogunda, coming in my humble
way, to visit with you for a little while
that we may gather some of the fruits of the
FAther's Garden of Knowledge, Inspiration,Love
and Light, that we may partake of the essence
of the greater glory of the Higher Self of
each and every one of us who are gathered here
together.

Sometimes I come to you only by remote
control, so to speak, but tonight I AM with
you in person, and in Spirit and in Love.
We shall be able I hope to be in perfect rapport one with the other and find our place
with other physical beings and by the side of
those Masters who have called us to their service.

We have all been called, although we may
not have heard, audibly that particular call.
There are many who do not recognize it as a
call. They do however recognize that "something" is drawing them upward and onward in
the service of the Kingdom of God and in a way
they cannot explain. This cannot be reasoned
or explained by the finite mind.

I did not intend to give you an introduction, but I do desire to welcome you here,
each and every one and commend you for your
faithfulness, not only in your attendance, but
in your meditation and acceptance of the messages that I give you.

There is quite a difference between an
intellectual acceptance of a message or a print
ed page and the heart or soul acceptance of that
message. I thank all of you who have accepted
both of them in a way which is very commendable.
I also thank all who have assisted in a marvel-
lous manner in many ways, not only in the re-
search, typing and gathering together of data,,
the dissemination and preparation of the magazine and in other ways which has come to your
minds.

Undoubtedly you are anticipating a Thanksgiving message from me this evening. I shall
not dissapoint you, for the subject of my discourse is three words: Gratitude, Thanksgiving
and Praise.

Perhaps I could have just taken one word,
for a subject, but I wanted to bring a broader
meaning to my words and thinking so that you
might grasp more completely the meaning of
Thanksgiving. Thanksgiving, of course, is a
National Holiday. It has sort of become a
more or less common event along with the other
Holidays, such as Christmas, New Years which is
observed by thousands very thoughtlessly with
the improper attitude toward the purpose for
which it was instituted.

I will start with the word, Gratitude.
Now there is some difference between Gratitude
and Thanksgiving. When you are grateful for
something which you have received, or which
some of your friends or relatives have received,
or which has been bestowed upon you, it is usually an attribute of the inner sanctum of the
soul, that which is beyond the outer form. So
you are grateful in your heart.

Your gratefulness may manifest itself in
some manner such as the giving of a gift, in-
viting someone for a visit, or in many other
ways.

The word, Thanksgiving has somewhat the same meaning, yet, some difference. When you give thanks, it is usually a vocalization of your gratitude. If you are grateful for something you have received or something you have accomplished, than you vocalize it, or you become very happy about it, and you give thanks for it.

Of course, sometimes, this is silent, but the word, Thanksgiving, has a connotation of vocal meaning because you are usually very meaningful about this and you tell your friends and neighbors about it.

The first Thanksgiving was instituted by the Pilgrim Fathers after they have become truly grateful for all the blessings they had received, and it was an outward manifestation of gratitude. They gathered together and had a great feast. At that time, the fowls which roamed the prairies were a very necessary part of their food and also they had all of the wonderful things to be thankful for -- their crops, their harvest and all of the many things with which they had been supplied. So, they gathered together and gave Thanks in outward form, and they set aside this day to be observed throughout posterity for their gratitude for the many blessings they had received.

So this a very solemn occasion, rather than one which is celebrated in a very boisterous and wild manner just as many celebrate the Christmas Season.

If you are grateful in your heart for all that you have received, express it orally as a Thanksgiving Message to your friends, to your relatives and to all about you.

Thanksgiving is a sequel to gratitude and is the outward expression of the gratitude within your heart which you give in a vocal manner. Now after you have Gratitude and Thanks-

giving, you perhaps might think this is enough.
and you stop there, but that is not all.

There is another quality which climaxes
the gratitude and thanksgiving which you have
in your heart, and that is Praise. This is the
praise that you give your Heavenly Father for
His benevolence. If you do not have all three
of these attributes, then you have not completely fulfilled the attitude and intent which was
in the minds of your forefathers when they instituted the Holiday of Thanksgiving.

Your praises should not only come from your
lips, but they should come from your heart as
well. This might be termed as "Thanks", but
it is of a higher octave, than simply "Thanks."
You thank people and every time you receive something you should say, "Thank you." This is as
it should be, but it is more of a "stereotyped"
term. So the observance of Thanksgiving has
become, in some ways, a "stereotyped" holiday.
Those who are truly grateful and those who are
thankful in their hearts, then follow up with
praise. Praise and Thanksgiving go together
for a grateful heart.

In the churches on Thanksgiving, they sing
praises and you can sing praises in heart even
if you cannot sing a note. You must give praise
when praise is due whether it is to your fellow
man, to your Heavenly Father or all the Spiritual Hierarchy who have been responsible for
bringing about many blessings that have been
bestowed upon you in the last year, since the
last Thanksgiving.

Since Thanksgiving is only an annual af-
fair, you should not wait until the season
comes around to be grateful, thankful or to
praise. It should be a continual manifestation of your every day life, every hour or ev-
ergy day. You may say, " I can't do that, I
have so many other things to do." This is true,

but your <u>attitude</u> can be one of gratefulness, thankfulness and praise for all of the blessings that have been bestowed upon you. If you will just try to count them, you will find it very difficult to enumerate all your blessings on a single page, or a whole book. You cannot count the blessings that have been bestowed upon you in this last year of your life -- none of you can, those who are now hearing my voice, nor those who listen to the tapes, or read these words. Your blessings are limitless.

Sometimes, you become discouraged and think that you do not have the blessings others have, and most certainly you do not because you do not have the same <u>kind</u>. If you did have the same kind, then you would all be alike and would have no need for Thanksgiving Day.

You have a day on which you can rest your souls and mind and relax and think about all the blessings. Of course, if you are preparing a great feast, then it will be more difficult for you to relax. To those who have to work on Thanksgiving Day, I would like to have you, just for a moment, think about your blessings and say a little decree in your innermost soul. Those who have to work on Thanksgiving Day, in preparing big feasts of which you, yourselves will partake, should be praised and you should be thankful to others for their praise, and you should be thankful you can serve in this manner. It should not be a chore for anyone, to prepare a feast, or anything which gives others pleasure.

One of the basic principles of Universal Love and Light is that you should find joy and gratitude, thanksgiving and priase in everything that you do for any other individual upon the face of the earth, whether they are your relatives or your friends, or strangers to you. Even if you have to sacrifice some of your own earthly pleasure momentarily for this job, it should be a work of Love, Service and Joy.

Thanksgiving should be enjoyed by all, although shadows are hanging over your own individual souls and over the earth, yet they should be forgotten for the time being and let a great wave of gratitude, thanksgiving and praise roll over your spirits in order that you may enjoy the day which has been set aside for your enjoyment and for your Thanksgiving, Gratitude and Praise.

I hope that I have given you something to think about as you partake of the festivities and pleasures of Thanksgiving Day among your relatives and friends, and even strangers. Make it a joyful day and forget about the shadows, even if they do hang over you individually or over the earth, itself, for you are yet underneath the everlasting arms; you are yet under an umbrella of light as I have given to you in the past. This umbrella of Light is over your Beloved City and protects it, and has protected it and will protect it yet for some time to come.

You have much more to be thankful for than the many thousands and even millions in other parts of the world, even in other parts of your nation.

Be thankful, grateful and sing praises unto the Father on High, for all He has given you. I AM thankful for all that He has given to me. I AM grateful for many, many things, not only in the fact that I can bring my humble messages to you to try to enlighten the darkened world, but I AM also grateful and give praise to the Almighty that I AM upon a plane or existence where shadows do not appear, except as I look into them and at them on a lower octave of my vibration.

Now you may ask questions.

Q: Thankyou, Master Yogunda. I have a scripture in mind which I would like to have you interpret for me. It reads like this: "Whatever you bind on earth, shall also be bound in Heaven." What does this mean?

A: Well, my Beloved Chelah, that is fairly simple. Yet, it would require many words to clarify it and to the extent which might term comprehensible. What does the word, "bind" mean? It has many meanings. The Hebrew meaning was rather the word was derived from the Hebrew word, Yea-ma-na. Yeamana, does not mean to bind in a physical body or form. It means that which binds you in your consciousness. For instance, if you are greatly enamoured, let us say, with certain individuals, certain organizations or certain material substance, which you have bound to yourself, then, of course, these will bind you when you pass over to the other side.

It does not mean that you are to bind someone with a rope, or something of that kind, for often your mind is bound. There are millions upon the earth ;whose minds are bound. Their minds are bound by creeds, traditions, teachings, by the cords of obstinacy or many other things. The word has a very broad meaning, and so you are bound to many things and you bind many things.

You are bound and you also bind others or things. You bind your physical possessions, your relatives, neighbors, friends to you and if you bind them too tightly, they will also be bound when you go to the other side. This is about as general an idea as I can give you. We could go into more detail, but whatever you bind here, will also be bound in the other world.

This does not mean that you should ignore everyone or everything as there is a vast difference between ignoring them and blessing them. You can use discretion and you can lead, follow and have the use of many, many things. You can

associate with your friends and relatives
without binding them. Does that not answer
your question for you?

Q: The thought comes to me -- what about the
relationship of man and wife? Does this law
include that relationship?

A: No, that is a different situation. This is
not binding. YourBeloved Saviour told you there
is no marriage in Heaven or the giving or re-
leasing in marriage. It is very rare, let us
say, where the man and wife land even upon the
same circle of the same plane, that is, unless
they are soul-mates or twin rays or they have
been assigned to work together. There are thousands who work together, not only in the Spiritual World but perhaps, even in the next incarnation. As a general rule, it does not apply
to the marriage relationship.

Q: Master Yogunda, in a recent lecture by Mel
Noel, he has told where he would return from
this so-called space journey. I wonder if you
could verify and give us some enlightenment upon it.

A: Yes, I can give you some information upon
it. There will be a slight delay in the take-
off. It will almost be on schedule and he will
return but not at the time which had been scheduled or the time contemplated. There wil be more
work and conferences than was anticipated in
the original plans. It is now anticipated that
he and the group will not return until a specific
time when it is necessary for them to assist in
another lift-off of another group in another
part of the world and this also was not anticipated at this particular time.

In making such a journey many things enter
into it which are in the Divine Plan and also
in the plan of the Space People who taking this
group. Mr. Noel will return and will seem to
be in the lapse of time it was intended to take.

Many have prepared for his return and he will
return in a very unconventional manner which
was not anticipated. I cannot give you detailed information. He will return even though
it was predicted he would not return. This
prediction was based on the fact that he
would not return in the specified time which
was allotted for them to be away. This is the
discrepancy.

Q: Master Yogunda, getting back to the question of evacuating people of the earth who
are the Chelahs and students trying to be of
the Light, would the families be included,
even though their families do not believe
in this information.

A: Now you have asked me a very difficult
question and I cannot give you a general answer. I could refer you to the Scripture where
it says, "Two will be in the field, and one
will be taken." Now, in many cases, the entire family will be taken. In other cases,
it will not be so. It will depend entirely
upon their spiritual progression. No, I will
use the word, "expediency" instead of progression. There will be many who shall be left
and taken to places of safety. They will not
be taken in space ships, except to deposit
them to places where they will be protected.
Then they shall be here to assist in the rehabilitation of those who need them. Many
will be taken to other places of habitation,
and I do not use the word, plenet exactly.
There is one particular place which I see
that has been prepared for some with lower
vibratory traits of those will be eventually
be prepared to return to the earth at a later
time.

There are two or three hundred categories which could be named in regard to
these people It is rather unfortunate that
these people have been divided into two or

three groups, for such is not the case. You
could not possibly take the population of several billion people and divide them only into
two or three groups? There will be hundreds
and hundreds of categories, but this has all
been arranged.

This is the reason there are thousands
and thousands of space craft under the Ash-
tar Command and these are only a part of them.
These have come from outside the Galaxy and
are really more informed about the duties that
will be performed than those who are close,
for they have had more experience in this sort
of evacuation. There are so many things which
could be spoken upon and which would become
somewhat involved.

Q: Will our Holy Bible become obsolete as
we know it? The Book of Revelations -- will
that become obsolete? Will there be a new
Bible written later?

a: There will be a new Bible written, but it
will not be Absolute as might be expected.
This new Bible is now in the process of preparation. It will be taken from many of the
Holy Books. However, that is another question, I might give you a discourse upon. You
will not depend upon any Holy Book.

The people of Venus do not have any Holy
Bible. They do not have a Holy Book. The Holy
Book is within the Holy Sanctum of their own
selves. They have their Sanctuary or their
Holy Book within their own Higher Selves which
is in complete rapport and harmony with their
lower selves. Eventually, people of the Earth
will have the same characteristics, but not
for several centuries. The manifestations
of it will be sooner of course. You have been
told that the New Age will come in the year
2000 AD. That is correct, it will come in
the year 2000 AD, but how could it have reached its fullness in such a short time? You are

a long way from the New Age. The New Age will
gradually dawn, and you will be like a new-
born baby. You will have to learn many things.
You may think you know much now, but you do
not know anything yet, so you will learn much
more aNd you will not have to wait until the
year 2000. You are learning much now and you
will learn more.   The New Age will come approximately the year 2000 or 2001. Then you will
have to grow and it will be a long time before you will be able to compare yourselves
with the inhabitants of Venus.

That is about all that I can tell you.
Thank you, so much.

Q: I know that if we are seeking spiritually,
our diet is important to our growth which will
mean following a vegetarian diet. With children, how would one gradually take away from
them meats. Could you tell me this in a few
words?

A: Yes, very definitely, My Beloved Chelah.
In regard to bringing up children -- this
could be a subject for a complete discourse.
Let me tall you briefly: If the father and
mother are already vegetarians, then, of course,
it is no probelm at all because they will not
have meat before them. It is not necessary
for them to eat meat. Growing children do not
need meat any more than you need meat. If they
are in a meat-eating family, they should not
be cut off meat abruptly. There should be a
gradual transition from meat to fish or sea-
food of some kind which, of course, is not ab-
solutely prohibited by any standards. Even the
eating of meat is an individual matter, but
those who want themselves to follow a vegetarian diet will gradually eliminate the meats.
Meat diets will be eliminated in the New Age.

It would be a mistake to try to suddenly
eliminate meat from the diet of a child or an
adult when they have been eating it all their

lives. I hope this answers your question.

Q: Please explain the difference between the Adamic Race and Israel?

A: There is a vast difference. The Adamic race was the first race that inhabited the earth which was procreated by the Angels who came from Heaven, in space ships, so to speak, and started the first race.

The Israelites are those who have progressed or graduated from the original sinful race which was the Adamic race. The Adamic Race was the original race and the Scriptures term it 'sinful' although they do not use that particular word. (All have sinned in Adam. Ed.). You are a part of Israel. Israel is composed of those people who have the Christ Light. This is as about as much as I can give you.

The Adamic Race were supposed to have guided the people of the earth, but instead they procreated with them , and that became the Adamic Race. There is much detail as to the reasons for this and the progenitors who followed.

The Israel Race is the race now upon the earth which is coming into its fullness and will be banded together. In fact, the Israel Race will be the ones to be taken into the Space Ships or who will be re-newed, or will be brought back to repopulate the earth after it has gone through its turmoil. This is the great difference between the Adamic and the Israel Races

I always like to give you any inspiration, encouragement and enlightenment which may come to me to give you, or which may come to your minds to inquire about. Your inquiries are the manifestions of active minds and souls and you are anxious to learn. What you are learning now will not have to be learned later.

Good night and God Bless you all.

*   *   *   *   *

- 64

Rest thou shalt find, O Soul, in the midst
of thyy sorrow, and thou shalt hold divinest
communion with kindred spirits. What more exal-
ting and uplifting experience than the communion
and fellowship of emancipated spirits. In sil-
ence, soul speaks to soul; thought leaps forth
without sound; intelligence is transmitted upon
the gentle waves of ether.

Then hast thou, O Soul, realized thy relationship with the Eternal Spirit. The spirit
of man is indestructible, his soul immortal, his
individuality everlasting, and therefore, let us
not mourn and lament over Death, for Death is
the Gateway to Life.

Benediction

May the understanding of our minds, the
meditation of our hearts and the obedience of
our will to the still small voice within, lead
us to live our spiritual life with fidelity and
fearlessness.   AMEN.

*   *   *   *   *

DEATH

Swing softly, beauteous gates of death,

to let a waiting soul pass on,

Achievement crowns life's purposes

And Victory is forever won.

Swing softly, softly, heavenly gate,

Thy portal passed, no more to roam,

Our traveler finds her journey o'er,

And rest at last in "Home Sweet

Home."

Alice B. Howe, Author.

NEWS ITEMS 65

The highlight of the activities for June
were the four wonderful days that Rev. Violet
Gilbert of Rainbow Temple, Santa Barbara, Cal.
spent with us at The Universariun Center. Her
days (and also part of the nights) from June
19 to June 22nd, were filled to overflowing
with physical, mental and spiritual instruction which she gave profusely to overflow seek-
ers both at the Center and the Public Lecture
on Wednesday, June 21st.

The average attendance at the classes
held here each afternoon was 19 and there
were approximately 300 in attendance at the
lecture. In addition to this, she gave private
readings here at the Center. She is one of
those individuals who draws energy from the
Cosmic Realms and her supply of this while
she was here was unlimited and uninhibited in
the Spiritual Vortex in which she works.

They will be unforgettable days by ye editor and hundreds who met and associated with
her while she was here.

Incidentally, a very marvelous "reading"
was given ye editor by Rev. Gilbert which in-
dicates that the Universariun Foundation, Inc.
will soon have a large Center with meeting
room, etc. not very far from its present loca-
tion. Those of you who are looking for us to
move to the vicinity of Yucca Valley or Timbukt
will be sadly dissapointed. We shall remain in
the vicinity of the most beautiful city in the
nation, Portland, Oregon, and the "safest"
place in the world for an indefinite period.
****

DIOPHANTES
Rev. Margaret Barnett of Fresno, Calif.
has sent out another spurious communication
in regard to Diophantes. She wrote to Fred &
Mary Robinson of Armadale, Australia that Diophantes had left the earth and been taken by

the Space People to help in the coming evacuation. About the time this was written he, and
his consort were in California and were giving a lecture to a small group at Rainbow
Temple in Santa Barbara. Subsequently, they
came back to Oregon and stayed in Portland
for more than a week, but by no means at the
Universariun Center. They are now in the
Seattle area.

About the time that Diophantes was lec-
turing in the Seattle Area and we were dis-
inheriting him, Rev. Barnett wrote to Reginald
Bradbury in Devon, England that Diophantes was
in Australia and would arrive in England on
an approximate date and then would come to
New York. Mr. Bradbury, unwittingly, scheduled Diophantes to speak tentatively at Caxton
Hall there. Subsequent knowledge of the facts
has caused Mr. Bradbury considerable embarrass-
ment.

The Church of the Golden Cross in Fresno
is defunct and Margaret Barnett cannot be
reached by conventional means. Her activities
along this line should be stopped if at all
possible.

****

FUTURE ISSUES

On page 3 of this issue, Master Yogunda
has given us an interpretation of the 11th
Chapter of the Book of Revelations. An earnest
request from the Group prompted him to make
arrangements with Sananda to continue these
interpretations. Therfore, on the following
Sunday, Beloved Sananda gave us the interpretation of the 12th Chapter and has promised to
interpret the entire Book for us. His message
on the 12th and 1st Chapter have been received
and will be published in the May 1967 issue.
This will be a very remarkable series. Don't
miss them!

Q: You mean, I will not return from my hospit-
alization?

A: I do not care to answer that question. You
will return, yes.

Q: I believe that is all of the questions this
evening, Master Yogunda.

A: I thank you, My Beloved Chelahs for listening and for your interest. God bless you each
and every one. I project to you both Love and
Prosperity that you may have all the necessities
and joys of life, now and forevermore. Amen.

*   *   *   *   *

BOOK LIST

"ICARUS, PRELUDE TO DOOM" and "SIRIUS II SPACE
SHIPS" are still available at 5 cents for the
two.

"O, URANTIA, WHITHER GOEST THOU?" (which contains
the above messages) and four or five others of
confirmation, is in limited supply at $2.00
each.

The 1966 Bound Volume of The Voice of Universarius is now available at $7.50.

*   *   *

THE BRIDGE
(Song)

Words by
Longfellow

Music By
Lady Carew

I stood on the bridge at midnight,
As the clocks were striking the hour,
And the moon rose o'er the city
Behind the dark church tow'r

Among the long black rafters
The wav'ring shadows lay;
And the current that came from the ocean
Seem'd to lift and bear them away.

As sweeping, eddying through them,
Rose the belated tide,
And streaming into the moonlight
The seaweed floated wide.

And like those waters rushing,
Among the wooden piers,
A flood of thoughts came o'er me
That fill'd my eyes with tears

How often! O how often, in the day
   that had gone by,
I had stood on that bridge at midnight
And gazed on that wave and sky.
How often! O how often I had wished that
   the ebbing tide
Would bear me away on its bosom
O'er the oceans wild and wide.

For my heart was hot and restless,
And my life was full of care;
And the burden laid upon me
Seemed greater than I could bear.

But now it has fallen from me,
It lies buried in the sea,
And only the sorrow of others
Throws the shadow over me.

And I think how many thousands
Of care : encumbered men,
Each bearing his burden of sorrows,
Have crossed the bridge since then.

Forever and forever,
As long as the river flows,
As long as the heart has passion,
As long as life has woes.

The moon and its broken reflection,
And its shadows shall appear
As the symbol of love in Heaven,
And its wav'ring image here.

—   —   —

Ed. Note: This poem by Henry Wadsworth Longfellow, set to music by Lady Carew of England
is a favorite of Zelrun Karsleigh and was sung
by him at one of Joseph Busby's lectures on
Busby's visit to Portland. Joseph Busby said
he knew Lady Carew very well and would convey
the information to her on his return to England
that his host had sung her song especially for
the Busby's.

We would appreciate hearing from anyone who has
copies of the song, The Bridge and also the
song, Plains of Peace, another of the old fav-
orites. These two songs are not catalogued.
They are out of print and cannot be purchased.
If anyone knows where copies of either of these
two songs can be secured, please write to the
Universariun Foundation, Inc.

BEYOND THE SUNSET

Sould you go first and I remain,
   to walk the road alone,
I'll live in memories garden, dear
   with happy days we've known.

In spring I'll wait for roses red,
   when faded, the lilacs blue.
 In early fall when brown leaves fall.
   I'll catch a glimpse of you.

Should you go first and I remain,
   for battles to be fought,
Each thing you've touched along the way
   will be a hallowed spot.

I'll hear your voice, I'll see your smile
   tho blindly I may grope,
The memory of your helping hand
   will buoy me on with hope.

Should you go first and I remain,
   one thing I'll have you do:
Walk slowly down that long, long path,
   for soon I shall follow you.

I want to know each step you take,
   so I may take the same,
For someday down that lonely road,
   you'll hear me call your name.

****
****
****

www.ingramcontent.com/pod-product-compliance
Lightning Source LLC
Chambersburg PA
CBHW070931270326
41927CB00011B/2809